JUL   2013

Dessert Designer

DECORATING AWESOME CAKES
PIECE of CAKE!

by Dana Meachen Rau

CAPSTONE PRESS
a capstone imprint

Snap Books are published by Capstone Press,
1710 Roe Crest Drive, North Mankato, Minnesota 56003.
www.capstonepub.com

Library of Congress Cataloging-in-Publication Data
Rau, Dana Meachen, 1971–
Piece of cake! : decorating awesome cakes / by Dana Meachen Rau.
p. cm.—(Snap books. Dessert designer)
Includes bibliographical references and index.
Summary: "Step-by-step instructions teach readers how to create
food art with cake"—Provided by publisher.
ISBN 978-1-4296-8618-1 (library binding)
ISBN 978-1-62065-341-8 (ebook pdf)
1. Cake decorating—Juvenile literature. I. Title.
TX771.2.R38 2013
641.86'539—dc23   2011051563

Editor: Jennifer Besel
Designer: Juliette Peters
Food and Photo Stylist: Brent Bentrott
Prop Preparation: Sarah Schuette
Scheduler: Marcy Morin
Production Specialist: Kathy McColley

Photo Credits:
All photos by Capstone Studio/Karon Dubke
except:
Tania McNaboe, p. 32 (author's photo)

Printed in the United States of America in
North Mankato, Minnesota.
042012   006682CGF12

Table of Contents

PARTY ON!

From birthdays to welcome-home parties, every occasion is better with cake. When you add your imagination, you can create a masterpiece people will cheer for!

Think of cakes as sculptures. But instead of clay, you'll be working with something much sweeter. Cakes come in a variety of flavors. And they can be circles, squares, or rectangles. To make your sweet sculpture, choose the best cake to fit your plan. You can make your own or buy an unfrosted cake at a bakery. And don't forget the toppings! Frosting and decorations add flavor and fun.

How to Use This Book

You'll find lots of project ideas in these pages. Follow the simple steps to create a sweet work of art.

Before you begin a project, read over the ingredient list. Make sure you have everything you need. You'll find most ingredients you need at the grocery store. Craft and hobby stores sell cake decorating tools. But your kitchen and pantry may already be a treasure chest of supplies.

The Best Part!

Some might argue that frosting is the most important part of a cake. Stores sell super-tasty tubs of premade frosting. But if you want to whip up your own, here's a simple recipe. It makes about 2½ cups (600 milliliters) of frosting.

~ Frosting ~

½ cup (120 mL) unsalted butter, softened to room temperature
½ teaspoon (2.5 mL) vanilla extract
2 cups (480 mL) confectioners' sugar
1 to 2 tablespoons (15–30 mL) milk

Steps

1. In a large bowl, cream the butter and vanilla with a mixer on medium speed until fluffy.
2. Beating on low, alternate adding sugar and milk until the ingredients are mixed well. The frosting should be thick, creamy, and spreadable.
3. Store the frosting in the refrigerator in an airtight container. Bring it to room temperature and rewhip before using.

For some cakes in this book, you'll need to make royal icing. Royal icing hardens into a firm shell so your cake has a smooth finish. There are two kinds of royal icing. Flood royal icing is thinner and good for filling in large areas. Edge icing is thicker and good for making details and edges.

~ EDGE Icing ~

2 teaspoons (10 mL) meringue powder
2 tablespoons (30 mL) water
2 to 2½ cups (480 to 600 mL) confectioner's sugar

With a mixer on high, blend the ingredients together in a bowl for about four to five minutes. The icing is the right consistency when it forms little peaks that hold their shape.

Makes 1 cup (240 mL) of icing

~ FLOOD Icing ~

Make a batch of edge icing. Then add water ½ teaspoon (2.5 mL) at a time, blending after each addition. The icing is ready when drips hold their shape for just a moment before they blend back into the icing.

~ Use Your Imagination ~

The ideas in this book are just that—ideas! Don't like a color or decoration we used? Change it! Can't find the same candy? Use something else. The best part of dessert designing is getting to be creative. Have fun!

DECORATOR'S TOOLBOX

A painter needs brushes and canvases. A carpenter needs hammers and nails. A cake decorator like you needs tools too!

~ wax paper ~
Use this supply to keep taffy and other sticky stuff from sticking to your workspace.

~ tweezers ~
Use tweezers to place those tiny decorations in just the right place.

~ spoons ~
Have a bunch of spoons ready to stir up a rainbow of frosting.

~ kitchen shears ~
These scissors are designed for use with food.

~ fondue fork ~
This tiny fork is great for dipping small pieces of cake into frosting.

~ turntable~
This spinning tool isn't necessary, but it is helpful. Turntables make it easy to frost all sides of a cake without accidently putting your elbows in it!

~ sharp knife ~
Have a few of these on hand to score candy or cut the cakes.

~ toothpicks and wooden skewers ~
These are great for helping keep layers together or to drag designs into frosting.

~ bowls ~
Keep a variety of these around to mix up frosting. Make sure that bowls used for melting candy are microwave safe.

~ cooling rack ~
Not only is this tool great for cooling goodies, but the slats let frosting drip off a project for a smooth finish.

~ piping bag ~
This fabric or plastic bag holds frosting and is used to decorate cakes and cupcakes.

~ zip-top bags ~
These make a great substitute for piping bags.

~ cutting board ~
Do any cutting on the cutting board to avoid damaging kitchen counters.

~ rolling pin ~
This is a handy tool for flattening taffies.

~ spreader ~
This might be the most handy decorating tool. Use it to cover surfaces with a smooth layer of frosting.

~ food coloring ~
Food coloring makes your frosting stand out. Just put a drop of liquid or a dab of gel into your frosting. You'll find a little goes a long way.

~ decorating tips ~
These go on the piping bag to create cool designs with frosting.

COASTER CAKE

Do you crave the sweet thrill of a roller coaster? Create the ups and downs with this very tasty attraction.

INGREDIENTS

1 8-inch (20-centimeter)
    square cake
2 9-inch (23-cm) round cakes
vanilla frosting
green, blue, and brown
    food coloring
red licorice whips
rainbow licorice twists
gum balls
pretzel sticks
8 teddy bear crackers
4 fun-size candy bars
4 pieces each of red and yellow
    candy-coated chewing gum
16 round candy necklace pieces

1. Cut one round cake in half. Cut the other cake so one half is slightly larger than the other.

2. Lay the square cake on your cake board. Place the two evenly cut cake halves at each end of the square cake.

3. Mix up a batch of green frosting. Frost the cakes on the board.

4. Mix up a batch of blue frosting. Place the unevenly cut cake halves side-by-side on top of the green cake. Frost these two pieces blue.

5. Mix up a batch of brown frosting. Pipe horizontal tracks up and down the blue cakes and around the green cake.

6. Place the licorice whips on each side of the tracks. Use kitchen shears to cut whips to the lengths needed.

7. Use rainbow licorice twists to decorate around the sides of the green cake and the sides of the blue hills. Use kitchen shears to cut these to the right lengths too.

8. Use a dab of frosting to glue a gum ball to the top of each licorice twist.

9. Gently press pretzel sticks to the sides of the blue hills to look like supports for the roller coaster.

10. Pipe green frosting on the tops of the candy bars to look like seats.

11. With a sharp knife, cut the legs off the bear crackers. Pipe a line of frosting on the bottom edges of two bears. Glue them in their frosting "seats" on a candy bar. Repeat with the other bears and candy bars.

12. Use frosting to glue the candy-coated gum pieces on the front and back of each car for lights. Then glue four candy necklace pieces to each car as wheels.

13. Place the cars in a line on the cake, setting the wheels in the frosting tracks.

Tip:
Experiment with different piping tips to get the look you want when decorating with frosting. Round tips are great for outlining details. Basket weave tips can make long, ribbed stripes.

~ Cake Boards ~

You'll need something to put your cake creations on. Cut a piece of cardboard the same size or a little bigger than your cake. Lay the board on a piece of aluminum foil. Cut the foil larger than the board. Fold the foil over the back of the cardboard and tape flat.

FOOLED YOU
PB&J

A sandwich for dessert? You bet! Transform a favorite lunchtime food into an unexpected, and delicious, dessert.

INGREDIENTS

2 ½-inch- (1-cm-) thick
 slices of pound cake
peanut butter
vanilla frosting
raspberry jam
1 piece each of green and
 orange taffy

Tip:

Peanut butter and jelly aren't the only sandwich spreads you could create.

• White frosting looks like cream cheese.

• Tan frosting and white candy wafers edged with green frosting look like hummus and cucumber.

• Yellow frosting and red fruit leather look like grilled cheese with bacon.

Get creative, and make a whole deli of desserts!

1. With a knife, cut each pound cake slice in half width wise.

2. Mix 2 tablespoons (30 mL) peanut butter into the vanilla frosting. Use a clean spoon to taste the frosting. If you want a more peanutty taste, add more peanut butter in small amounts until it's just right.

3. Generously spread the peanut butter frosting on two halves of the "bread."

4. Spread jam on the other two halves.

5. Place the frosting and jam slices together.

6. For a pickle to put on the side, roll the green taffy between your hands to get a pickle shape. Then round the ends. Use a toothpick to poke small holes up and down the taffy.

7. To make carrots, flatten the taffy between sheets of wax paper with a rolling pin. Cut out strips that are about ½ inch (1 cm) wide. Gently press fork tines into the strip to make crinkles.

POOL PARTY

Nothing beats a relaxing day of poolside fun—except cake! Dive into this supersweet treat any time of year.

INGREDIENTS
blue gelatin
2 9x13-inch (23x33-cm)
    rectangular cakes
vanilla frosting
blue and yellow food coloring
blue and red taffy
1 stick chewing gum
yellow and red fruit leather
4 round breath mints

1. Make a batch of blue gelatin according to the package directions. Place it in the refrigerator. When it is halfway through its hardening time, take it out and stir it up with a spoon. Return to refrigerator to finish hardening.

2. Place one of the cakes on your cake board. Cut out a rectangle from the middle of the other cake. Set the removed rectangle of cake aside.

3. Spread frosting on top of the cake on the board. Place the cut cake on top. Mix up a batch of light blue frosting. Frost the top of the cake and the inside of the rectangle with blue frosting.

4. Mix up a batch of yellow frosting. Pipe the yellow frosting up the sides of the cake in wide, overlapping strips.

5. Spoon gelatin into the hole until it reaches the top to fill up your pool.

6. Warm the blue taffy in the microwave for about 5 seconds. Place it between two pieces of wax paper and roll it flat with a rolling pin. With kitchen shears, cut the flat taffy into 1-inch (2.5-cm) squares. Keep rolling and cutting taffy into squares until you have about 62 of them. Place them all around your pool, like tiles on a pool deck.

7. Pipe a wide line of yellow frosting around the edge of the pool.

8. To make a diving board, stack two pieces of red taffy at the edge of the pool. Glue on a stick of gum with a bit of frosting.

9. Cut a triangle from the removed center piece of cake. Cover with blue frosting. With a kitchen shears, cut a strip of yellow fruit leather to lay over the triangle for a slide. Press two round mints to the sides to look like railings. Place the slide near one corner of the pool.

10. Flatten pieces of red and blue taffy. Roll each into long, thin ropes. Then wrap the red rope around the blue rope. Put a short length of the rope on the pool deck. Use longer taffy ropes to decorate the outer edge of the cake.

11. Cut small strips of red fruit leather. Wrap the strips around the mints for life rings. Place on the pool deck.

Tip:
Experiment with different candies to make other pool toppers. Green taffy can be molded to look like flippers. Gumdrops and gummy candies make excellent chairs. And sour candy belts make great beach towels.

BOX OF CHOCOLATES

Is it a box of chocolates? Is it a cake? It's both! Give two treats in one with this cake your friends will love.

INGREDIENTS

2 8-inch (20-cm) square cakes
vanilla frosting
pink, purple, green, and brown
    food coloring
a box of chocolates
    with about 16 pieces

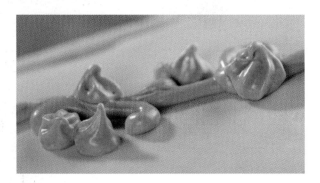

Tips:

• For parts that need to be sturdy, professionals frost cake boards and Styrofoam instead of cake. Just be sure to warn your guests not to eat it!

• Level cakes so they'll lay flat when you stack them. With the cake at eye level, place your knife at the edge and skim it through the top of the cake. This cut will take off the higher middle part.

1. Level your cakes so the tops are flat. Place one cake on the cake board

2. Mix up a batch of pink frosting and frost the top of the cake on the board.

3. Cut a square out of the middle of the second cake, leaving just a 2-inch (5-cm) frame. Place the frame of cake on top of the frosted cake.

4. Cut an 8-inch (20-cm) square of cardboard. Cover it with aluminum foil and tape the foil to the back. This will be the "lid" of your box.

5. Frost the entire cake with pink frosting, including the inside of the hole. Also frost the top and edges of the cardboard square.

6. Open your real box of chocolates. Place the chocolates inside the hole of the cake.

7. Mix up batches of purple, green, and brown frosting. Pipe accents on the box and lid. Write a message on the lid. Be creative and have fun.

8. Gently set your lid at an angle against the cake to look like someone snuck into your box of chocolates.

TIE-DYE T-SHIRT

Get groovy with this retro cake. Set a food fashion trend with this tie-dye creation!

INGREDIENTS

1 9x13-inch (23x33 cm)
   rectangular cake
1 8-inch (20-cm) square cake
vanilla frosting
rainbow sprinkles
edge royal icing (see page 5)
flood royal icing (see page 5)
red, blue, yellow, and green
   food coloring

1. Trim out a half circle from one short end of the rectangular cake. This is the shirt collar.

2. Cut two sleeve shapes out of the square cake. Glue the sleeve pieces to the larger cake with some frosting.

3. Level the cakes so the top is completely flat.

4. Frost the top and sides of the cake with vanilla frosting. Press rainbow sprinkles onto the sides all around the cake.

5. Place the cake in the refrigerator for 30 minutes to firm up the frosting.

6. Meanwhile, mix up a batch of white edge icing and put in a piping bag.

7. Divide the flood icing into five bowls. Tint four of the bowls red, yellow, green, and blue. Leave one bowl white. Put each color in a separate piping bag.

8. Pipe white edge icing around the top edges of the cake. Then spoon white flood icing onto the cake. Spread icing with the back of the spoon to cover the top.

9. Starting in the middle of the cake, pipe a swirl of red flood icing. Continue the swirl to the outer edge of the cake. Don't forget to do the sleeves.

10. Pipe a yellow swirl next to the red swirl, leaving some white space between them.

11. Pipe a green swirl next to the yellow swirl. Then do a blue swirl.

12. While the flood icing is still wet, pull a toothpick through the icings. Pull the toothpick in a curved line from the center to the outside edge. Continue all around the cake to create a tie-dye effect.

13. Let the cake sit for a few hours to let the frosting harden.

ROCKIN' GUITAR

Plug into this sweet treat and get ready for a rocking good time. This electric guitar will pump up the volume of fun at your next party.

INGREDIENTS

2 9-inch (23-cm) round cakes
pink, orange, and yellow
    food coloring
vanilla frosting
edge royal icing (see page 5)
flood royal icing (see page 5)
1 dark chocolate bar,
    broken in pieces
3 long chocolate wafer candies
12 sugar pearls
3 round chocolate-covered mints
1 round brown candy-coated chocolate
chocolate melting wafers

1. Make a template of the shapes needed to make a guitar. Use them to cut shapes out of the cakes. Glue the pieces together with a little frosting on your board.

2. Level the top of the cake.

3. Mix up a batch of pink frosting. Spread over the top and sides of the cake. Pipe beads of frosting around the bottom edge. Place the cake in the refrigerator until the frosting gets firm, about 30 minutes.

4. Mix up a batch of edge royal icing. Color it pink to match your frosting.

5. Mix up a batch of flood royal icing. Divide into three bowls. Color one bowl orange, one yellow, and one pink.

6. With the pink edge icing, pipe a line around the top edge of the entire cake.

7. Spoon the pink flood icing onto the cake top to completely cover the cake.

8. While the pink flood icing is still wet, pipe yellow and orange flame shapes on the body of the guitar.

9. Let the icing harden for an hour.

10. When the icing has hardened slightly, but not completely set, place on the candy details. Place six chocolate bar pieces on the neck of the guitar.

11. Place two long chocolate candies in the middle of the body. Place another long chocolate candy at the top of the neck.

12. Align six sugar pearls along the bottom edge of the last long chocolate candy on the body. Put six pearls along the left edge of the top of the guitar.

13. Place three chocolate-covered mints and one candy-coated chocolate along the right side of the body.

14. Place a few melting wafers in a small zip-top bag. Leave the bag open and microwave on the defrost setting for 30 seconds. Squeeze the melted candy to one corner. If the wafers are not soft yet, microwave on defrost 30 seconds more. Then snip a small corner off the bag.

15. On a piece of wax paper, pipe six strings of chocolate, long enough to go from the top of the neck to the body. Let them harden for an hour. Then place them on the cake.

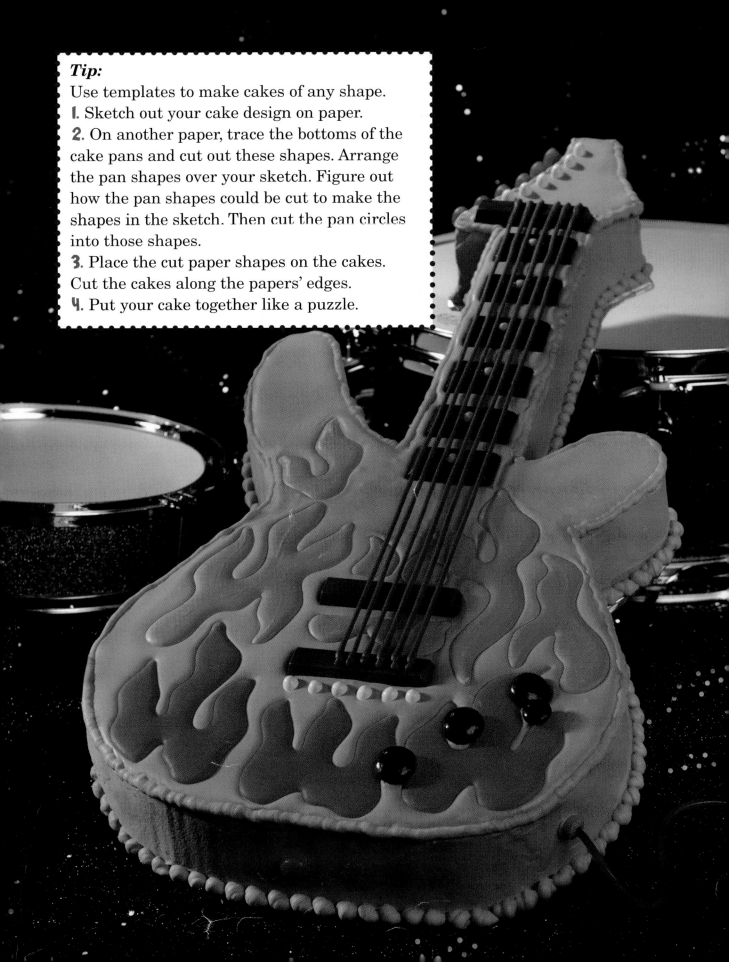

Tip:
Use templates to make cakes of any shape.
1. Sketch out your cake design on paper.
2. On another paper, trace the bottoms of the cake pans and cut out these shapes. Arrange the pan shapes over your sketch. Figure out how the pan shapes could be cut to make the shapes in the sketch. Then cut the pan circles into those shapes.
3. Place the cut paper shapes on the cakes. Cut the cakes along the papers' edges.
4. Put your cake together like a puzzle.

mini mice

Tiny mice have snuck into the kitchen to snatch some cheese. Create these cake critters for your next party, and guests will snatch them up.

INGREDIENTS
1 10.75-ounce (305-gram) frozen
    pound cake
chocolate frosting
5 chocolate kisses
10 sliced almonds
5 cherry stems
yellow and red food coloring
vanilla frosting
edge royal icing (see page 5)

1. With a melon baller, scoop out five balls from the cake.

2. Put the chocolate frosting in a microwave-safe bowl. Heat for about 15 seconds in the microwave. Stir. You want the frosting to be a liquid, pourable consistency. Heat another 15 seconds if it is still too thick.

3. Prepare your work surface by placing a piece of wax paper under a cooling rack.

4. Stick a ball of cake on a fondue fork. Swirl the ball in the chocolate frosting until it is well covered. Tap the fork onto the side of the bowl so the excess frosting drips off.

5. With a butter knife, push the ball off the fork onto the cooling rack. The extra frosting will drip down onto the wax paper.

6. While the icing is still wet, stick a chocolate kiss to the ball as a head. Poke two sliced almonds on top as ears. Stick a cherry stem to the back as a tail.

7. Repeat steps 4–6 with the rest of the cake balls. Let the mice sit for a few hours until the icing hardens.

8. Cut a wedge out of the leftover pound cake. With the melon baller, scoop out holes from the wedge's surface.

9. Mix up a batch of yellow frosting. Heat it in the microwave as in step 2.

10. Dip the wedge into the yellow frosting as in step 4, and transfer to the cooling rack. Let harden.

11. Pipe small dots of white frosting on the mice as eyes. Pipe chocolate frosting on as eyebrows.

12. Mix up a batch of red edge royal icing. Put it in a piping bag. Pipe a small red nose at the tip of each chocolate kiss.

These little bites of cake are called petit fours. Petit four is French for "small oven."

enchanting
PEACOCK

Peacocks are elegant and stylish birds. They are also a surprising cake creation. Make this cake to reflect your glamorous, enchanting, and unique personality.

INGREDIENTS
edge royal icing (see page 5)
blue, orange, yellow, green,
    and black food coloring
35–40 oval-shaped cookies
4 tablespoons (60 mL) butter
    (plus some extra)
1 bag mini marshmallows
6 cups (1,440 mL)
    crispy rice cereal
3 9-inch (23-cm) round cakes
vanilla frosting
1 white candy wafer

1. Make a batch of edge icing and divide into five bowls. Tint the icing in each bowl so you have dark blue, light blue, orange, yellow, and green.

2. Pipe a dark blue heart shape on one end of each cookie. Let icing set until hard.

3. Next pipe a blue circle around the heart. Then pipe a large orange oval around the blue.

4. Pipe a yellow edge around the orange icing. Finally end with green around the cookie's edge. Feel free to get creative with the design of your cookies. When you're done let the cookies sit for a few hours.

5. Lay out a piece of wax paper. On the paper, pipe the icings into the shape of a peacock's crest of head feathers. Let it sit on the wax paper for a few hours.

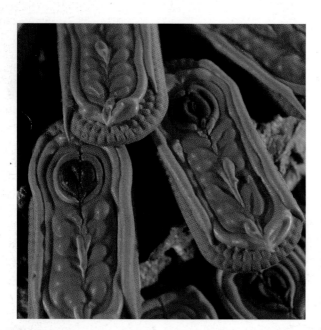

CONTINUED ON NEXT PAGE

6. With an adult's help, melt 4 tablespoons (60 mL) butter on medium heat in a large pot. Add the bag of marshmallows. Stir until they melt. Remove the pot from the heat, and pour in the cereal. Mix well.

7. Cover your workspace with a piece of wax paper. Coat it with some butter. Empty the pot of marshmallow treats onto the paper. Let it cool slightly. Rub butter all over your hands. Then mold the cereal into a head and neck shape.

8. Place the head into the refrigerator to harden for about 30 minutes.

9. Make a template of your three round cakes. Using the head as a guide, draw arches of cake to fit against the head in three steps. The bottom layer should be the biggest layer and the top the smallest. Use the templates to cut your cakes.

10. Place the crispy rice head on the cake board. Then place the bottom cake pieces against the head. Place the middle cake on top of that. Finally add the third layer. Trim the cakes as needed to make them fit against the head without too many gaps between.

11. Mix up a batch of blue frosting. Frost the head and body. On the head and neck, make small upward strokes with the spreader to make the frosting look like feathers.

12. Press cookies into the outside edge of the bottom cake. Space them as evenly as possible.

13. Add a second layer of cookies on top of the bottom cake. Offset the cookies a bit so they aren't directly above the cookies on the first layer.

14. Add three more layers of cookies, covering your peacock with feathers.

15. Arrange the icing crest on top of the peacock's head.

16. Mix a small batch of black frosting. Pipe a small eye on each side of the peacock's head.

17. Score the candy wafer with a knife. Then snap it in half along the line. Place one half on each side of the peacock's head just under the eye.

18. Use black and white frosting to add details to the eyes and nose.

MANI-PEDI DRESSER

Get the girls together for a spa night! Do your nails, braid your hair, and eat cake. What could be better than that?

INGREDIENTS

1 cake ball
1 black licorice twist, cut in half
pink, blue, and chocolate
    melting wafers
2 pieces hard stick candy
2 8-inch (20-cm) square cakes
chocolate frosting
vanilla frosting
1 chocolate bar
about 20 pink round candies

1. Make a cake ball from the recipe on the next page. Mold a spoonful of cake ball dough around one half of a licorice twist to make a nail polish bottle. Freeze the bottle for about an hour.

2. Melt the pink melting wafers according to package directions. Holding the licorice stem, dip the bottle into the melted candy. Set on wax paper to harden.

3. Draw a simple picture of a hand mirror on a piece of paper. Place a piece of wax paper over it.

4. Place a few blue melting wafers in a small zip-top bag. Leave the bag open and microwave on the defrost setting for 30 seconds. Squeeze the melted candy to one corner. If the wafers are not soft yet, microwave on defrost 30 seconds more. Then snip off a small corner of the bag.

5. Trace over your mirror drawing with the melted candy on the wax paper. If you wish, drizzle white or chocolate melted candy on the blue to create a design. Let the mirror harden.

6. Dip one side of a hard candy stick into the melted pink candy. Dip the second stick in the melted blue candy. Set both on wax paper to harden.

7. Level your cakes. Then glue the two layers together with frosting. Frost the entire cake with chocolate frosting.

8. Pipe vanilla frosting on the top to look like a lacy doily.

9. Break the chocolate bar along its ridges to create two rectangles. Glue them to the cake front with a dab of frosting. Pipe a small blob of vanilla frosting in the center of each rectangle to make drawers.

10. Place the bottle, mirror, and nail files on top of the cake.

11. Arrange the pink round candies on the cake to look like a necklace.

Cake balls are easy to make and tasty to eat. Make a nail polish bottle cake ball for everyone at the spa party.

Ingredients
One rectangular cake or two rounds.
One tub of frosting

Crumble the cake into a bowl so there are no large pieces. Then add one spoonful of frosting at a time. Mix well after each addition. Your mixture should be a moist dough that you can mold into balls. If it seems too dry and falls apart easily, add more frosting. You'll probably use most of a tub of frosting.

ZEBRA·STRIPED PURSE

Animal prints may reveal your wild side. But with so much frosting, you can't help being sweet too!

INGREDIENTS

2 8-inch (20-cm) square cakes
vanilla frosting
black and pink food coloring
2 red licorice twists
4 round breath mints
1 mini chocolate bar

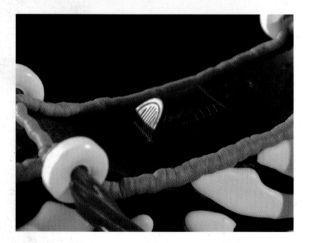

Tip:
Want to make a different shaped purse? Here are some ideas.
Clutch: Cut the cake in half to make a cordless clutch.
Satchel: Use two-thirds of the cake to make a satchel with small handles.

1. Glue the flat sides of the two cakes together with a layer of frosting. On each corner, poke a straw all the way through both layers. Trim off the extra straw that sticks out. These straws will help keep the layers together.

2. Cut a small semi-circle from one side of the cake, keeping the corners intact. This will be the top of the purse. Spread a little frosting on the opposite end, then stand the cake up on the cake board.

3. Mix up a batch of black frosting. Use it to frost all the sides of the cake.

4. Pipe outlines of white stripes across the sides of the cake. Then pipe more white frosting inside the outlines. Smooth out with a spreader.

5. Mix up a batch of pink icing. Pipe the pink frosting along the edges and base of the purse.

6. Thread each licorice twist through the holes of two mints. Carefully stick the mints on the purse to make handles.

7. Place the chocolate bar on top of the purse to make a clasp.

INGREDIENTS GLOSSARY

fruit leather

rainbow
licorice twists

teddy bear
crackers

oval-shaped
cookies

rainbow
sprinkles

sugar pearls

round breath
mints

pink round
candies

round
chocolate-covered
mints

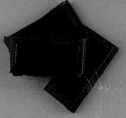

dark chocolate
bar in pieces

candy melting
wafers

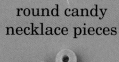

candy-coated
chewing gum

round candy
necklace pieces

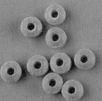

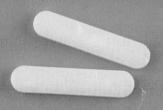

hard stick
candy

red licorice whips

chocolate kisses

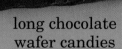

long chocolate wafer candies

sliced almonds

taffy

TERMS GLOSSARY

consistency (kuhn-SIS-tuhn-see)—how thick or thin something is

excess (EK-sess)—extra

pipe (PIPE)—to make details by squeezing frosting from a bag

score (SKOR)—to make a straight line or groove on a flat surface

template (TEM-plate)—a pattern used to cut out cake shapes

tint (TINT)—to color slightly

Read more

Maurer, Tracy. *Cupcakes, Cookies, and Cakes.* Creative Crafts for Kids. Vero Beach, Fla.: Rourke Pub., 2010.

Rau, Dana Meachen. *What's Up, Cupcake? Creating Amazing Cupcakes.* Dessert Designer. North Mankato, Minn.: Capstone Press, 2013.

Tuminelly, Nancy. *Cool Cake & Cupcake Food Art: Easy Recipes that Make Food Fun to Eat!* Cool Food Art. Edina, Minn.: ABDO Pub., 2011.

Internet Sites

FactHound offers a safe, fun way to find Internet sites related to this book. All of the sites on FactHound have been researched by our staff.

Here's all you do:
Visit *www.facthound.com*
Type in this code: 9781429686181

About the Author

Dana Meachen Rau writes about many topics, including food! When she's not writing, she's being creative in other ways—especially in the kitchen. Sometimes she follows recipes, but other times she experiments with new flavors. And she doesn't need a special occasion to whip up a special dessert for her friends and family in Burlington, Connecticut.

Super-cool stuff! Check out projects, games and lots more at **www.capstonekids.com**